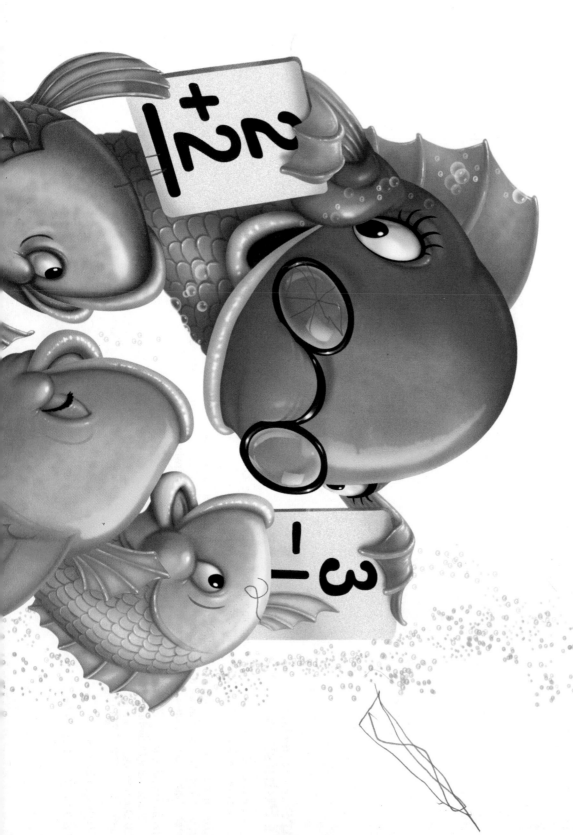

I Can
Add and Subtract

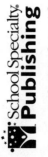

Name _M a d i p_

Add.

```
  4          2          9          8
 +3         +2         +1         +7
  7          4         10         15
```

```
  4          1          3          3
 +6         +8         +0         +8
 10         9          3         11
```

```
  5          7          9          7
 +7         +2         +6         +2
 12         9         15          9
```

```
  7          4
 +3         +5
 10          9
```

3

Add.

Name _Maja k_

```
  0        4        9        4        1
 +3       +7       +2       +6       +0
 ___      ___      ___      ___      ___
  3                                   1
```

```
  4        8        9        6        7
 +8       +9       +2       +2       +4
 ___      ___      ___      ___      ___
```

```
  7        9        8        9        6
 +3       +5       +4       +3       +7
 ___      ___      ___      ___      ___
  6
```

```
  7        0        4
 +3       +2       +4
 ___      ___      ___
  6        2        8
```

Add.

Name _____

$$\begin{array}{r}6\\+4\\\hline 10\end{array}\qquad\begin{array}{r}9\\+9\\\hline 18\end{array}\qquad\begin{array}{r}7\\+5\\\hline 12\end{array}\qquad\begin{array}{r}6\\+2\\\hline 8\end{array}\qquad\begin{array}{r}1\\+3\\\hline 4\end{array}$$

$$\begin{array}{r}7\\+7\\\hline 14\end{array}\qquad\begin{array}{r}8\\+4\\\hline 12\end{array}\qquad\begin{array}{r}3\\+3\\\hline 6\end{array}\qquad\begin{array}{r}5\\+1\\\hline 6\end{array}\qquad\begin{array}{r}4\\+8\\\hline 12\end{array}$$

$$\begin{array}{r}5\\+8\\\hline 13\end{array}\qquad\begin{array}{r}6\\+0\\\hline 6\end{array}\qquad\begin{array}{r}0\\+3\\\hline 3\end{array}\qquad\begin{array}{r}5\\+6\\\hline 11\end{array}\qquad\begin{array}{r}8\\+5\\\hline 13\end{array}$$

5

Addition

Add.

Name _____

$$\begin{array}{r} 6 \\ +3 \\ \hline \end{array} \qquad \begin{array}{r} 0 \\ +0 \\ \hline \end{array} \qquad \begin{array}{r} 3 \\ +2 \\ \hline \end{array} \qquad \begin{array}{r} 3 \\ +3 \\ \hline \end{array} \qquad \begin{array}{r} 9 \\ +7 \\ \hline \end{array} \qquad \begin{array}{r} 5 \\ +9 \\ \hline \end{array}$$

$$\begin{array}{r} 3 \\ +8 \\ \hline \end{array} \qquad \begin{array}{r} 3 \\ +6 \\ \hline \end{array} \qquad \begin{array}{r} 8 \\ +0 \\ \hline \end{array} \qquad \begin{array}{r} 7 \\ +9 \\ \hline \end{array} \qquad \begin{array}{r} 4 \\ +6 \\ \hline \end{array} \qquad \begin{array}{r} 0 \\ +6 \\ \hline \end{array}$$

$$\begin{array}{r} 9 \\ +1 \\ \hline \end{array} \qquad \begin{array}{r} 6 \\ +9 \\ \hline \end{array} \qquad \begin{array}{r} 7 \\ +7 \\ \hline \end{array} \qquad \begin{array}{r} 4 \\ +9 \\ \hline \end{array}$$

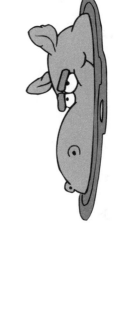

6

Add.

Name _____

```
  3       9       8       5       6       0
+ 6     + 5     + 9     + 2     + 7     + 4
```
9 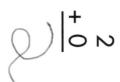 14

```
  2       3       8
+ 0     + 7     + 5
```
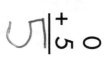

```
  4       3       3
+ 8     + 7     + 7
```

```
          0       8       4       3       6
        + 5     + 1     + 4     + 6     + 8
```
5

Add.

Name _____

5 +2	6 +0	8 +8
5 +5	7 +7	2 +6
0 +7	6 +6	8 +3

4 +4	0 +7
0 +3	3 +7
4 +1	4 +7
	8 +9

Add.

Name _____

5 + 9 =   1 + 3 =   8 + 9 =   5 + 0 =   7 + 6 =

1 + 1 =   4 + 5 =   8 + 2 =   3 + 5 =   3 + 9 =

7 + 4 =   9 + 4 =   2 + 8 =   5 + 7 =   8 + 2 =

9 + 5 =   0 + 0 =   7 + 5 =

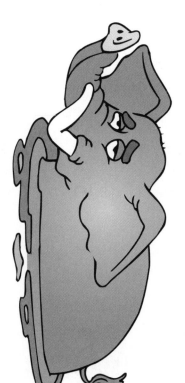

Addition

Add.

Name _____

4 + 4 =	1 + 3 =	6 + 2 =	8 + 0 =	6 + 5 =

3 + 3 =   2 + 1 =   9 + 3 =   6 + 8 =   3 + 6 =

3 + 9 =   8 + 7 =   6 + 5 =   4 + 8 =   8 + 3 =

2 + 7 =   5 + 3 =   8 + 9 =

10

Name _____

Add.

6 + 7 =   3 + 1 =   9 + 7 =   0 + 0 =

6 + 0 =   7 + 7 =   4 + 3 =   6 + 5 =

8 + 1 =   8 + 8 =   5 + 4 =   5 + 3 =

4 + 5 =   8 + 3 =   4 + 7 =   3 + 8 =

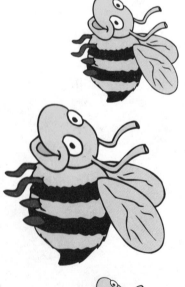

Addition

Add.

Addition ➕

5 + 8 =	2 + 1 =	3 + 2 =
		9 + 0 =
2 + 8 =	4 + 4 =	9 + 7 =
		6 + 5 =
4 + 3 =	6 + 5 =	9 + 2 =
		3 + 6 =
		2 + 1 =
7 + 7 =	3 + 3 =	6 + 5 =

Addition

Add.

Name _____

3 + 3 = 3 + 7 = 4 + 2 = 3 + 1 = 9 + 4 =

1 + 7 = 4 + 8 = 3 + 7 = 6 + 3 = 4 + 7 =

5 + 8 = 9 + 4 = 5 + 2 = 3 + 8 = 5 + 5 =

8 + 4 = 6 + 6 = 9 + 5 =

Addition

Add.

Name _____

1 + 6 =	4 + 5 =	9 + 6 =	4 + 8 =
4 + 2 =	8 + 4 =	4 + 6 =	8 + 5 =
7 + 8 =	0 + 5 =	1 + 2 =	0 + 3 =
9 + 2 =	5 + 8 =	6 + 6 =	5 + 7 =

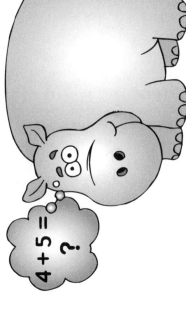

4 + 5 = ?

Name _____

Add.

4 + 2 =   6 + 8 =   4 + 8 =   7 + 2 =   7 + 0 =

$$\begin{array}{r} 6 \\ + 8 \\ \hline \end{array}$$
$$\begin{array}{r} 9 \\ + 3 \\ \hline \end{array}$$
$$\begin{array}{r} 0 \\ + 0 \\ \hline \end{array}$$
$$\begin{array}{r} 2 \\ + 4 \\ \hline \end{array}$$
$$\begin{array}{r} 6 \\ + 7 \\ \hline \end{array}$$
$$\begin{array}{r} 2 \\ + 7 \\ \hline \end{array}$$

5 + 8 =   1 + 1 =   3 + 6 =

Add.

Name _____

7 + 4 =

9 + 9 =

4 + 4 =

2 + 2 =

8 + 0 =

$\begin{array}{r} 3 \\ + 3 \\ \hline \end{array}$

$\begin{array}{r} 7 \\ + 9 \\ \hline \end{array}$

$\begin{array}{r} 5 \\ + 3 \\ \hline \end{array}$

$\begin{array}{r} 6 \\ + 9 \\ \hline \end{array}$

$\begin{array}{r} 6 \\ + 0 \\ \hline \end{array}$

$\begin{array}{r} 7 \\ + 8 \\ \hline \end{array}$

2 + 7 =

1 + 7 =

4 + 3 =

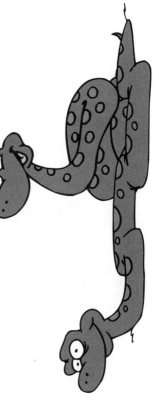

Addition Word Problems

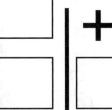

Addition

Solve each problem.

Ken sees 2 birds.

Pam sees 3 birds.

How many birds in all?

$$\begin{array}{r} 2 \\ +\ 3 \\ \hline 5 \end{array}$$

Bob has 3 cups.

George has 8 cups.

How many cups in all?

Patty has 1 car.

Kathy has 2 cars.

How many cars in all?

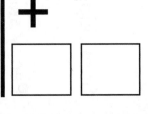

Bob has 7 pennies.

Lindsay has 9 pennies.

How many pennies in all?

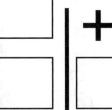

Name _____

Solve each problem.

Matt sees 5 planes.

Roger sees 9 planes.

How many planes in all?

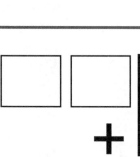

Sam skipped 8 rocks.

Penny skipped 7 rocks.

How many rocks in all?

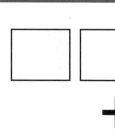

Mary has 2 marbles.

Tracy has 5 marbles.

How many marbles in all?

Barb has 4 dollars.

Carrie has 2 dollars.

How many dollars in all?

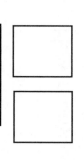

Name _____

Solve each problem.

Dave has 5 pencils.

Chris has 0 pencils.

How many pencils in all?

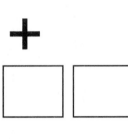

Amy has 2 watches.

Pam has 1 watch.

How many watches in all?

Ryan has 9 baseball cards.

Rick has 9 baseball cards.

How many cards in all?

Ted has 3 cats.

Laney has 7 cats.

How many cats in all?

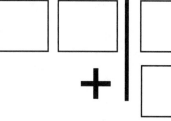

Solve each problem.

Name _____

Molly has 1 doll.

Clyde has 3 dolls.

How many dolls in all?

Kathy sees 8 leaves.

Emily sees 5 leaves.

How many leaves in all?

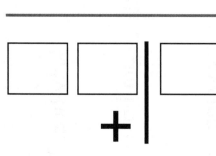

Eric has 6 toy trucks.

Josh has 8 toy trucks.

How many toy trucks in all?

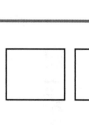

Carl sees 3 bottles.

Lenny sees 8 bottles.

How many bottles in all?

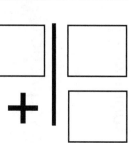

Name _____

Solve each problem.

Beth has 2 combs.

Pam has 7 combs.

How many combs in all?

Grace has 5 dresses.

Karen has 8 dresses.

How many dresses in all?

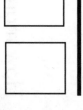

Samantha has 1 dog.

Susan has 2 dogs.

How many dogs in all?

Keith has 3 games.

Roger has 9 games.

How many games in all?

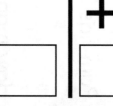

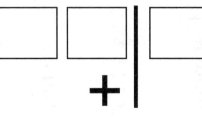

Solve each problem.

Name _____

Sue has 2 children.

Pam has 3 children.

How many children in all?

Catherine saw 6 movies.

Jonathan saw 4 movies.

How many movies in all?

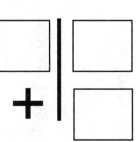

Ken sees 2 bugs.

Chris sees 9 bugs.

How many bugs in all?

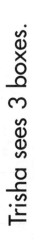

Jennifer sees 5 boxes.

Trisha sees 3 boxes.

How many boxes in all?

Name _____

Add.

```
  4 5        1 4        9 1        2 5
+   2      +   7      +   4      +   3
```

```
  3 8        9 5        3 8        7 2
+   0      +   9      +   4      +   6
```

```
  7 4        3 5        2 6        1 5
+   0      +   6      +   0      +   5
```

```
             4 4        9 1        9 8
           +   8      +   4      +   1
```

```
             3 7
           +   6
```

Add.

Name _____

1 5 + 5	4 8 + 4	9 5 + 3	9 3 + 6
			2 8 + 6
3 3 + 7	7 1 + 0	4 2 + 8	2 5 + 3
			7 3 + 7
8 2 + 5	4 2 + 7	2 7 + 8	3 7 + 5
			1 0 + 3
			4 1 + 6

WATERING HOLE

24

Name _____

Add.

$$
\begin{array}{r}
7\ 2 \\
+\ \ 5 \\
\hline
\end{array}
\qquad
\begin{array}{r}
1\ 8 \\
+\ \ 4 \\
\hline
\end{array}
\qquad
\begin{array}{r}
8\ 3 \\
+\ \ 6 \\
\hline
\end{array}
\qquad
\begin{array}{r}
8\ 1 \\
+\ \ 8 \\
\hline
\end{array}
\qquad
\begin{array}{r}
8\ 4 \\
+\ \ 4 \\
\hline
\end{array}
$$

$$
\begin{array}{r}
5\ 5 \\
+\ \ 0 \\
\hline
\end{array}
\qquad
\begin{array}{r}
2\ 9 \\
+\ \ 1 \\
\hline
\end{array}
\qquad
\begin{array}{r}
2\ 5 \\
+\ \ 7 \\
\hline
\end{array}
\qquad
\begin{array}{r}
4\ 0 \\
+\ \ 6 \\
\hline
\end{array}
\qquad
\begin{array}{r}
2\ 6 \\
+\ \ 3 \\
\hline
\end{array}
$$

$$
\begin{array}{r}
1\ 1 \\
+\ \ 2 \\
\hline
\end{array}
\qquad
\begin{array}{r}
6\ 2 \\
+\ \ 7 \\
\hline
\end{array}
\qquad
\begin{array}{r}
6\ 0 \\
+\ \ 9 \\
\hline
\end{array}
\qquad
\begin{array}{r}
8\ 8 \\
+\ \ 3 \\
\hline
\end{array}
\qquad
\begin{array}{r}
4\ 9 \\
+\ \ 0 \\
\hline
\end{array}
\qquad
\begin{array}{r}
3\ 5 \\
+\ \ 2 \\
\hline
\end{array}
$$

Addition

Name _____

31 + 6	72 + 9	28 + 4	93 + 8	40 + 3

41 + 5	15 + 0	46 + 2	29 + 6	34 + 9

18 + 7	63 + 8	91 + 7	55 + 6	79 + 5

94
+ 3

Name _____

Add.

$$
\begin{array}{r} 5\ 2 \\ +\ \ 7 \\ \hline \end{array}
\qquad
\begin{array}{r} 4\ 7 \\ +\ \ 8 \\ \hline \end{array}
\qquad
\begin{array}{r} 1\ 2 \\ +\ \ 0 \\ \hline \end{array}
\qquad
\begin{array}{r} 5\ 2 \\ +\ \ 8 \\ \hline \end{array}
\qquad
\begin{array}{r} 4\ 6 \\ +\ \ 7 \\ \hline \end{array}
\qquad
\begin{array}{r} 4\ 6 \\ +\ \ 6 \\ \hline \end{array}
$$

$$
\begin{array}{r} 6\ 3 \\ +\ \ 8 \\ \hline \end{array}
\qquad
\begin{array}{r} 2\ 7 \\ +\ \ 0 \\ \hline \end{array}
\qquad
\begin{array}{r} 6\ 7 \\ +\ \ 9 \\ \hline \end{array}
\qquad
\begin{array}{r} 1\ 9 \\ +\ \ 3 \\ \hline \end{array}
\qquad
\begin{array}{r} 2\ 3 \\ +\ \ 9 \\ \hline \end{array}
\qquad
\begin{array}{r} 8\ 4 \\ +\ \ 5 \\ \hline \end{array}
$$

$$
\begin{array}{r} 1\ 1 \\ +\ \ 6 \\ \hline \end{array}
\qquad
\begin{array}{r} 3\ 6 \\ +\ \ 8 \\ \hline \end{array}
\qquad
\begin{array}{r} 1\ 5 \\ +\ \ 8 \\ \hline \end{array}
\qquad
\begin{array}{r} 7\ 7 \\ +\ \ 7 \\ \hline \end{array}
$$

Addition

Add.

Name ___

```
  3 7        1 8        4 5        9 3        2 9        2 5
+   8      +   5      +   7      +   6      +   0      +   6
-----      -----      -----      -----      -----      -----

  2 5        2 7        4 0        4 6        5 3        6 3
+   3      +   4      +   2      +   8      +   6      +   7
-----      -----      -----      -----      -----      -----

  7 8        2 3        1 7        1 0
+   3      +   4      +   7      +   4
-----      -----      -----      -----
```

Add.

Name _____

27 + 9 =   14 + 8 =   54 + 2 =   11 + 9 =

25 + 3 =   94 + 8 =   84 + 1 = 85   36 + 0 =   72 + 7 =

84 + 1 =   77 + 8 =   65 + 4 =   97 + 1 =   47 + 3 =

55 + 0 =   86 + 2 =   50 + 8 =

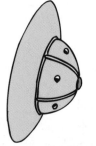

Addition

Add.

Name _____

63 + 9 =	20 + 1 =	85 + 8 =	20 + 6 =	90 + 3 =

55 + 9 =   56 + 9 =   69 + 6 =   92 + 8 =   72 + 4 =

27 + 8 =   11 + 1 =   81 + 8 =   46 + 2 =   97 + 0 =

73 + 1 =   40 + 2 =   16 + 5 =

Add.

Name _____

29 + 4 =   84 + 1 =   63 + 9 =   84 + 8 =   19 + 6 =

44 + 8 =   45 + 2 =   12 + 6 =   73 + 0 =   48 + 2 =

49 + 0 =   13 + 9 =   74 + 3 =   94 + 1 =   88 + 9 =

80 + 1 =   22 + 3 =   87 + 1 =

Add.

Name _____

85 + 1 =	74 + 0 =	33 + 1 =	84 + 0 =	67 + 3 =
59 + 1 =	22 + 0 =	29 + 4 =	51 + 7 =	14 + 9 =
94 + 4 =	14 + 0 =	38 + 1 =	99 + 1 =	34 + 7 =
33 + 9 =	52 + 4 =	65 + 9 =		

Add.

Name _____

56 + 9 =

82 + 7 =

64 + 3 =

62 + 7 =

34 + 5 =

95 + 2 =

35 + 4 =

30 + 5 =

72 + 4 =

46 + 8 =

57 + 7 =

19 + 9 =

56 + 7 =

43 + 9 =

60 + 7 =

33 + 5 =

61 + 0 =

90 + 1 =

Addition

+ Addition

Add.

Name _____

90 + 7 =	98 + 0 =	55 + 3 =
60 + 5 =	82 + 7 =	
64 + 6 =	63 + 7 =	67 + 0 =
25 + 9 =	91 + 5 =	
37 + 1 =	79 + 3 =	91 + 7 =
37 + 6 =	62 + 7 =	
10 + 3 =	36 + 5 =	
19 + 5 =		

Name _____

Add.

12 + 4 =   92 + 7 =   71 + 9 =   52 + 2 =   64 + 7 =

$$\begin{array}{r} 5\ 1 \\ +\ 6 \\ \hline \end{array}$$ $$\begin{array}{r} 2\ 8 \\ +\ 5 \\ \hline \end{array}$$ $$\begin{array}{r} 9\ 1 \\ +\ 3 \\ \hline \end{array}$$ $$\begin{array}{r} 4\ 7 \\ +\ 3 \\ \hline \end{array}$$ $$\begin{array}{r} 4\ 9 \\ +\ 0 \\ \hline \end{array}$$

86 + 4 =   14 + 0 =   37 + 7 =

$$\begin{array}{r} 1\ 3 \\ +\ 2 \\ \hline \end{array}$$

Add.

Name _____

94 + 1 =

62 + 8 =

38 + 2 =

40 + 1 =

82 + 9 =

```
  6 4
+   7
-----
```

```
  3 7
+   8
-----
```

```
  8 3
+   1
-----
```

```
  4 9
+   0
-----
```

```
  6 5
+   3
-----
```

```
  3 7
+   5
-----
```

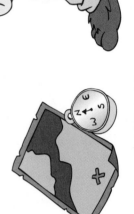

35 + 9 =

61 + 0 =

87 + 8 =

Solve each problem.

Ken sees 25 cars.

Pam sees 8 cars.

How many cars in all?

2	5
+	8
3	3

Fred sees 37 ants.

George sees 8 ants.

How many ants in all?

3	7
+	8

Ashley has 87 pens.

Sue has 0 pens.

How many pens in all?

+	

Tammy has 66 cars.

Sam has 7 cars.

How many cars in all?

+	

Addition Word Problems

Solve each problem.

Ryan has 12 balls.

Chris has 8 balls.

How many balls in all?

Ben has 48 dimes.

Pam has 5 dimes.

How many dimes in all?

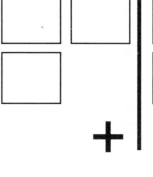

Terry has 22 balloons.

Penny has 7 balloons.

How many balloons in all?

Rachel has 14 rings.

Grace has 6 rings.

How many rings in all?

Name _____

Solve each problem.

Tommy has 11 pets.

Chris has 2 pets.

How many pets in all?

$$+$$

Tracey has 62 flowers.

Pam has 1 flower.

How many flowers in all?

$$+$$

Jen ran 12 miles.

Brenda ran 9 miles.

How many miles in all?

$$+$$

Joe did 74 pushups.

Rob did 9 pushups.

How many pushups in all?

$$+$$

39

Addition Word Problems

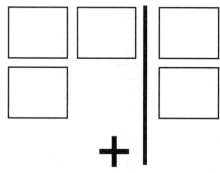

Solve each problem.

Name _____

Connie has 11 plums.

Pam has 1 plum.

How many plums in all?

☐☐ ☐
☐☐   ☐
   + |

Clark has 24 puppies.

David has 8 puppies.

How many puppies in all?

☐☐ ☐
☐☐   ☐
   + |

Beth has 47 keys.

Vivian has 4 keys.

How many keys in all?

☐☐ ☐
☐☐   ☐
   + |

Pam has 35 trucks.

Keith has 7 trucks.

How many trucks in all?

☐☐ ☐
☐☐   ☐
   + |

Solve each problem.

Name _____

Al has 14 games.

Rob has 8 games.

How many games in all?

 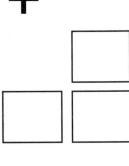

George reads 11 hours.

Ray reads 2 hours.

How many hours in all?

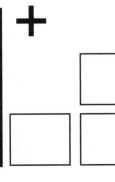

Kathy has 46 recipes.

Ben has 5 recipes.

How many recipes in all?

 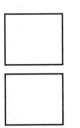

Robert has 83 movies.

Matt has 3 movies.

How many movies in all?

Addition Word Problems

Solve each problem.

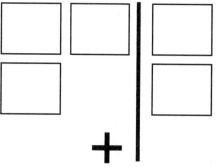

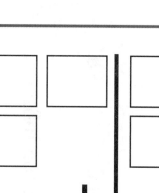

Eileen walked 20 miles.

Kathy walked 7 miles.

How many miles in all?

Ken sees 25 mice.

Pam sees 8 mice.

How many mice in all?

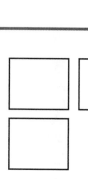

Ben sees 48 trees.

Ron sees 3 trees.

How many trees in all?

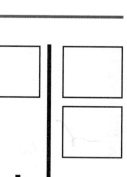

Oliver sleeps 11 hours.

Clyde sleeps 4 hours.

How many hours in all?

Add.

Name _____

$$\begin{array}{r} 3\ 4 \\ +\ 5\ 8 \\ \hline \end{array}$$

$$\begin{array}{r} 3\ 4 \\ +\ 7\ 7 \\ \hline \end{array}$$

$$\begin{array}{r} 1\ 6 \\ +\ 1\ 8 \\ \hline \end{array}$$

$$\begin{array}{r} 8\ 5 \\ +\ 7\ 4 \\ \hline \end{array}$$

$$\begin{array}{r} 4\ 3 \\ +\ 8\ 2 \\ \hline \end{array}$$

$$\begin{array}{r} 4\ 3 \\ +\ 3\ 7 \\ \hline \end{array}$$

$$\begin{array}{r} 1\ 9 \\ +\ 8\ 4 \\ \hline \end{array}$$

$$\begin{array}{r} 2\ 6 \\ +\ 3\ 9 \\ \hline \end{array}$$

$$\begin{array}{r} 9\ 3 \\ +\ 2\ 0 \\ \hline \end{array}$$

$$\begin{array}{r} 4\ 2 \\ +\ 4\ 8 \\ \hline \end{array}$$

$$\begin{array}{r} 2\ 7 \\ +\ 1\ 3 \\ \hline \end{array}$$

$$\begin{array}{r} 2\ 5 \\ +\ 6\ 6 \\ \hline \end{array}$$

$$\begin{array}{r} 8\ 3 \\ +\ 8\ 6 \\ \hline \end{array}$$

$$\begin{array}{r} 1\ 7 \\ +\ 5\ 3 \\ \hline \end{array}$$

$$\begin{array}{r} 6\ 8 \\ +\ 4\ 2 \\ \hline \end{array}$$

$$\begin{array}{r} 1\ 8 \\ +\ 6\ 5 \\ \hline \end{array}$$

Addition

Name _____

Add.

56 +10	93 +26	21 +27	23 +38	75 +42
				21 +18

83 +48	31 +47	53 +87	64 +38	47 +73
				84 +33

15 +37	47 +68	38 +79	28 +13

44

+ Addition

Add.   Name _____

$$\begin{array}{r}65\\+71\\\hline\end{array}$$ $$\begin{array}{r}35\\+78\\\hline\end{array}$$ $$\begin{array}{r}63\\+37\\\hline\end{array}$$ $$\begin{array}{r}65\\+42\\\hline\end{array}$$ $$\begin{array}{r}36\\+24\\\hline\end{array}$$ $$\begin{array}{r}62\\+48\\\hline\end{array}$$

$$\begin{array}{r}77\\+53\\\hline\end{array}$$ $$\begin{array}{r}73\\+71\\\hline\end{array}$$ $$\begin{array}{r}13\\+67\\\hline\end{array}$$ $$\begin{array}{r}13\\+40\\\hline\end{array}$$ $$\begin{array}{r}85\\+27\\\hline\end{array}$$ $$\begin{array}{r}91\\+30\\\hline\end{array}$$

$$\begin{array}{r}53\\+38\\\hline\end{array}$$ $$\begin{array}{r}93\\+90\\\hline\end{array}$$ $$\begin{array}{r}83\\+48\\\hline\end{array}$$ $$\begin{array}{r}50\\+35\\\hline\end{array}$$

Add.

Name _____

Addition +

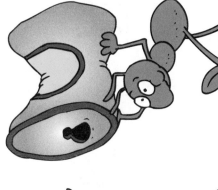

$$\begin{array}{r} 2\,5 \\ +\,3\,7 \\ \hline \end{array} \qquad \begin{array}{r} 1\,7 \\ +\,4\,6 \\ \hline \end{array} \qquad \begin{array}{r} 1\,6 \\ +\,3\,3 \\ \hline \end{array} \qquad \begin{array}{r} 1\,1 \\ +\,3\,7 \\ \hline \end{array} \qquad \begin{array}{r} 2\,5 \\ +\,2\,1 \\ \hline \end{array}$$

$$\begin{array}{r} 8\,1 \\ +\,5\,0 \\ \hline \end{array} \qquad \begin{array}{r} 7\,5 \\ +\,3\,2 \\ \hline \end{array} \qquad \begin{array}{r} 4\,2 \\ +\,6\,7 \\ \hline \end{array} \qquad \begin{array}{r} 8\,2 \\ +\,4\,8 \\ \hline \end{array} \qquad \begin{array}{r} 9\,1 \\ +\,3\,5 \\ \hline \end{array}$$

$$\begin{array}{r} 9\,4 \\ +\,3\,5 \\ \hline \end{array} \qquad \begin{array}{r} 8\,9 \\ +\,5\,1 \\ \hline \end{array} \qquad \begin{array}{r} 4\,4 \\ +\,4\,8 \\ \hline \end{array} \qquad \begin{array}{r} 4\,2 \\ +\,8\,1 \\ \hline \end{array} \qquad \begin{array}{r} 8\,3 \\ +\,4\,2 \\ \hline \end{array}$$

Add.

Name _____

$$\begin{array}{r} 2\ 7 \\ +\ 7\ 8 \\ \hline \end{array}$$

$$\begin{array}{r} 7\ 3 \\ +\ 3\ 1 \\ \hline \end{array}$$

$$\begin{array}{r} 1\ 8 \\ +\ 5\ 7 \\ \hline \end{array}$$

$$\begin{array}{r} 7\ 2 \\ +\ 3\ 8 \\ \hline \end{array}$$

$$\begin{array}{r} 4\ 1 \\ +\ 8\ 0 \\ \hline \end{array}$$

$$\begin{array}{r} 2\ 1 \\ +\ 5\ 8 \\ \hline \end{array}$$

$$\begin{array}{r} 7\ 4 \\ +\ 9\ 0 \\ \hline \end{array}$$

$$\begin{array}{r} 6\ 7 \\ +\ 3\ 0 \\ \hline \end{array}$$

$$\begin{array}{r} 5\ 7 \\ +\ 2\ 2 \\ \hline \end{array}$$

$$\begin{array}{r} 1\ 5 \\ +\ 8\ 2 \\ \hline \end{array}$$

$$\begin{array}{r} 4\ 1 \\ +\ 7\ 9 \\ \hline \end{array}$$

$$\begin{array}{r} 4\ 2 \\ +\ 5\ 7 \\ \hline \end{array}$$

$$\begin{array}{r} 1\ 4 \\ +\ 3\ 8 \\ \hline \end{array}$$

$$\begin{array}{r} 4\ 8 \\ +\ 7\ 3 \\ \hline \end{array}$$

$$\begin{array}{r} 9\ 1 \\ +\ 3\ 8 \\ \hline \end{array}$$

$$\begin{array}{r} 5\ 2 \\ +\ 2\ 9 \\ \hline \end{array}$$

47

Addition

Add.

Name _____

3 4 + 7 8	5 2 + 3 8	9 0 + 9 4	1 5 + 7 2	5 7 + 4 8	9 4 + 3 1

8 3 + 3 3	7 2 + 5 8	6 4 + 8 8	8 3 + 5 9	7 2 + 3 5	1 5 + 4 2

2 8 + 2 3	6 3 + 3 5	7 4 + 2 7	9 0 + 5 3

Name _____

Add.

26 + 84 =   87 + 35 =   61 + 44 =   14 + 10 =

50 + 43 =   82 + 43 =   71 + 87 =   62 + 85 =

11 + 53 =   83 + 67 =   97 + 16 =   66 + 19 =   57 + 73 =

16 + 52 =   75 + 94 =   83 + 10 =

Station

49

Addition

Add.

Name _____

66 + 73 =

71 + 10 =

93 + 97 =

77 + 64 =

51 + 11 =

14 + 14 =

64 + 22 =

81 + 61 =

54 + 73 =

43 + 66 =

61 + 47 =

91 + 10 =

60 + 71 =

10 + 12 =

34 + 19 =

Addition

Name _____

Add.

51 + 24 =   71 + 16 =   26 + 17 =   52 + 42 =

81 + 12 =   70 + 11 =   62 + 48 =   18 + 37 =   61 + 73 =

56 + 72 =   81 + 10 =   13 + 21 =   65 + 59 =   13 + 67 =

68 + 22 =   11 + 84 =   81 + 76 =

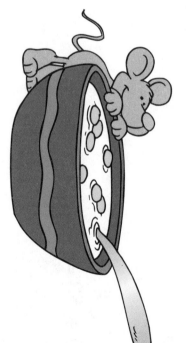

Add.

Name _____

84 + 62 =	72 + 56 =	33 + 41 =	71 + 86 =	90 + 19 =
56 + 47 =	31 + 10 =		64 + 84 =	12 + 47 =
64 + 51 =	59 + 13 =	57 + 61 =	37 + 22 =
10 + 53 =	12 + 43 =	86 + 71 =	69 + 75 =

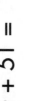

Add.

Name _____

17 + 22 =   61 + 72 =   84 + 90 =   56 + 71 =   31 + 58 =

35 + 86 =   23 + 75 =   56 + 58 =   89 + 24 =   46 + 97 =

35 + 48 =   53 + 80 =   97 + 37 =   60 + 12 =   53 + 79 =

45 + 78 =   79 + 24 =   14 + 24 =

Addition

Add.

26 + 84 =	56 + 90 =	34 + 79 =
36 + 73 =	67 + 87 =	
19 + 23 =	78 + 46 =	58 + 97 =
55 + 14 =	84 + 60 =	
26 + 84 =	72 + 60 =	67 + 80 =
73 + 82 =	10 + 54 =	
61 + 34 =	45 + 46 =	
78 + 21 =		

Add.

Name _____

51 + 46 =   25 + 79 =   67 + 43 =   54 + 97 =   64 + 10 =

```
  6 7          4 5          1 8          3 7          1 4          3 8
+ 3 8        + 3 2        + 8 4        + 8 9        + 4 1        + 5 0
```

19 + 72 =   82 + 36 =   47 + 25 =

Add.

Name _____

Addition

$84 + 60 =$

$10 + 15 =$

$83 + 72 =$

$49 + 38 =$

$50 + 24 =$

```
  7 3
+ 9 7
```

```
  4 5
+ 8 1
```

```
  8 9
+ 5 3
```

```
  5 0
+ 9 6
```

```
  1 4
+ 9 8
```

```
  4 5
+ 8 3
```

$76 + 14 =$

$90 + 36 =$

$45 + 27 =$

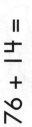

Name _____

Solve each problem.

Ken sees 25 birds.

Pam sees 20 birds.

How many birds in all?

$$\begin{array}{r} 2\;5 \\ +\;2\;0 \\ \hline 4\;5 \end{array}$$

Rachel has 88 marbles.

Paul has 75 marbles.

How many marbles in all?

Sam has 11 rabbits.

Paul has 25 rabbits.

How many rabbits in all?

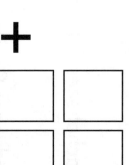

Jim has 53 coins.

Dan has 87 coins.

How many coins in all?

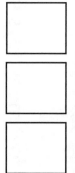

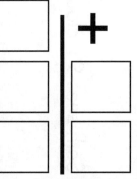

Addition

Solve each problem.

Name _____

Danny has 78 toys.

Tommy has 64 toys.

How many toys in all?

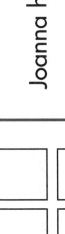

Rachel sees 38 clouds.

Seth sees 91 clouds.

How many clouds in all?

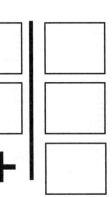

Joanna has 11 puppies.

Steve has 37 puppies.

How many puppies in all?

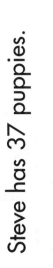

Randy has 48 pretzels.

Sandy has 62 pretzels.

How many pretzels in all?

Addition Word Problems

Solve each problem.

Donna sees 38 cats.

Rachel sees 61 cats.

How many cats in all?

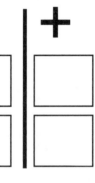

Dorthy has 10 ribbons.

Stacey has 12 ribbons.

How many ribbons in all?

Chris has 29 pencils.

Bob has 48 pencils.

How many pencils in all?

Ken sees 73 people.

Pat sees 48 people.

How many people in all?

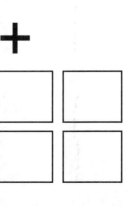

Addition Word Problems

Name _____

Solve each problem.

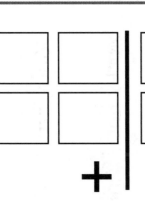

Ruth has 39 candles.

Sam has 27 candles.

How many candles in all?

Robert sees 36 bugs.

Doug sees 72 bugs.

How many bugs in all?

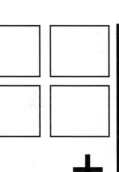

Matt ran 10 miles.

Dawn ran 13 miles.

How many miles in all?

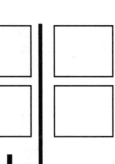

Greg has 31 bags.

Rob has 48 bags.

How many bags in all?

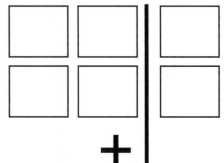

Solve each problem.

Name _____

Dave has 20 hats.

Andy has 52 hats.

How many hats in all?

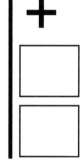

Corey has 73 cards.

Mandy has 35 cards.

How many cards in all?

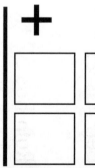

Ryan sees 14 kites.

Amy sees 36 kites.

How many kites in all?

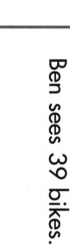

Paige sees 10 bikes.

Ben sees 39 bikes.

How many bikes in all?

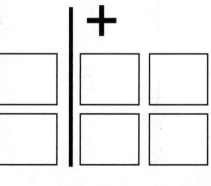

Addition Word Problems

Addition ➕

Name _____

Solve each problem.

Ben has 29 twigs.

Ruth has 52 twigs.

How many twigs in all?

$$
\begin{array}{r}
2\,9 \\
+\;5\,2 \\
\hline
8\,0 \\
\end{array}
$$ twigs

Kyle has 38 tapes.

Jason has 63 tapes.

How many tapes in all?

$$
\begin{array}{r}
3\,8 \\
+\;6\,9 \\
\hline
1\,0\,1 \\
\end{array}
$$ tapes

Brenda sees 86 people.

Pam sees 65 people.

How many people in all?

$$
\begin{array}{r}
8\,6 \\
+\;9\,5 \\
\hline
1\,5\,1 \\
\end{array}
$$ people

Craig sees 73 cars.

Joe sees 10 cars.

How many cars in all?

$$
\begin{array}{r}
7\,3 \\
+\;1\,0 \\
\hline
8\,3 \\
\end{array}
$$

Subtract.   Name _____

```
   8      4      7      9
 - 8    - 3    - 3    - 2
```

```
                           1
                         - 0
```

```
   6      7      8      9
 - 2    - 7    - 1    - 6
```

```
                    7      4
                  - 4    - 4
```

```
   1      8      7      9
 - 1    - 6    - 3    - 6
```

```
                    8
                  - 3
```

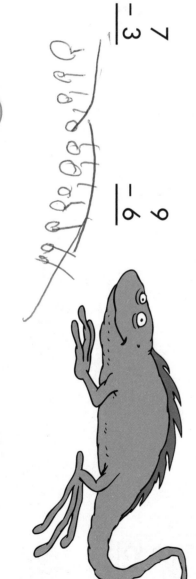

Subtraction

Name _____

Subtract.

9 − 9	8 − 3	5 − 3	9 − 0	7 − 5
5 − 2	9 − 1	6 − 1	6 − 5	1 − 1
8 − 5	4 − 4	8 − 4	8 − 2	6 − 6
				5 − 4

Name _____

Subtract.

$$\begin{array}{r} 2 \\ -2 \\ \hline \end{array} \qquad \begin{array}{r} 9 \\ -7 \\ \hline \end{array} \qquad \begin{array}{r} 9 \\ -5 \\ \hline \end{array} \qquad \begin{array}{r} 3 \\ -1 \\ \hline \end{array} \qquad \begin{array}{r} 8 \\ -4 \\ \hline \end{array} \qquad \begin{array}{r} 6 \\ -0 \\ \hline \end{array}$$

$$\begin{array}{r} 5 \\ -1 \\ \hline \end{array} \qquad \begin{array}{r} 6 \\ -3 \\ \hline \end{array} \qquad \begin{array}{r} 8 \\ -0 \\ \hline \end{array} \qquad \begin{array}{r} 9 \\ -6 \\ \hline \end{array} \qquad \begin{array}{r} 2 \\ -2 \\ \hline \end{array} \qquad \begin{array}{r} 7 \\ -3 \\ \hline \end{array}$$

$$\begin{array}{r} 7 \\ -4 \\ \hline \end{array} \qquad \begin{array}{r} 6 \\ -1 \\ \hline \end{array} \qquad \begin{array}{r} 7 \\ -5 \\ \hline \end{array} \qquad \begin{array}{r} 6 \\ -4 \\ \hline \end{array}$$

65

Name _____

Subtract.

6 − 3	8 − 7	7 − 6	8 − 1	7 − 1
7 − 1	9 − 4	5 − 2	4 − 3	6 − 6
7 − 3	5 − 4	8 − 5	7 − 2	0 − 0

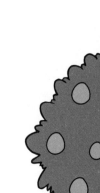

Subtract.

Name _pad y_

$$\begin{array}{r} 5 \\ -3 \\ \hline 2 \end{array} \qquad \begin{array}{r} 7 \\ -2 \\ \hline 5 \end{array} \qquad \begin{array}{r} 5 \\ -2 \\ \hline 3 \end{array} \qquad \begin{array}{r} 8 \\ -6 \\ \hline 2 \end{array} \qquad \begin{array}{r} 9 \\ -5 \\ \hline 4 \end{array}$$

$$\begin{array}{r} 5 \\ -5 \\ \hline 0 \end{array} \qquad \begin{array}{r} 6 \\ -6 \\ \hline 0 \end{array} \qquad \begin{array}{r} 1 \\ -1 \\ \hline 0 \end{array} \qquad \begin{array}{r} 7 \\ -4 \\ \hline 3 \end{array} \qquad \begin{array}{r} 8 \\ -8 \\ \hline 0 \end{array}$$

$$\begin{array}{r} 6 \\ -4 \\ \hline \end{array} \qquad \begin{array}{r} 1 \\ -0 \\ \hline 1 \end{array} \qquad \begin{array}{r} 7 \\ -0 \\ \hline 7 \end{array} \qquad \begin{array}{r} 3 \\ -3 \\ \hline 0 \end{array} \qquad \begin{array}{r} 5 \\ -2 \\ \hline 3 \end{array} \qquad \begin{array}{r} 7 \\ -4 \\ \hline 3 \end{array}$$

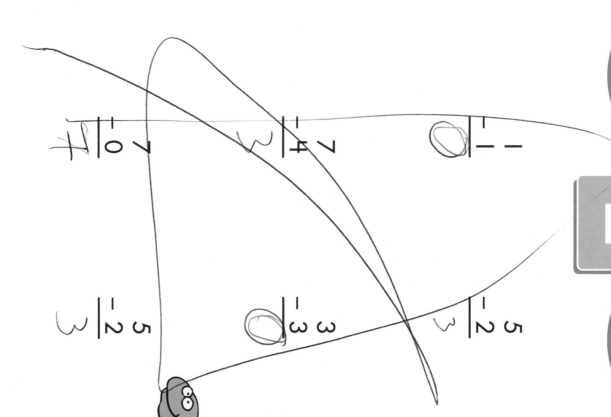

Subtract.

Name _____

$$\begin{array}{r} 8 \\ -5 \\ \hline \end{array}$$
$$\begin{array}{r} 2 \\ -1 \\ \hline \end{array}$$
$$\begin{array}{r} 1 \\ -1 \\ \hline \end{array}$$
$$\begin{array}{r} 5 \\ -1 \\ \hline \end{array}$$
$$\begin{array}{r} 7 \\ -5 \\ \hline \end{array}$$
$$\begin{array}{r} 5 \\ -3 \\ \hline \end{array}$$

$$\begin{array}{r} 4 \\ -1 \\ \hline \end{array}$$
$$\begin{array}{r} 7 \\ -3 \\ \hline \end{array}$$
$$\begin{array}{r} 5 \\ -5 \\ \hline \end{array}$$
$$\begin{array}{r} 7 \\ -0 \\ \hline \end{array}$$
$$\begin{array}{r} 9 \\ -9 \\ \hline \end{array}$$
$$\begin{array}{r} 8 \\ -8 \\ \hline \end{array}$$

$$\begin{array}{r} 3 \\ -3 \\ \hline \end{array}$$
$$\begin{array}{r} 0 \\ -0 \\ \hline \end{array}$$
$$\begin{array}{r} 6 \\ -3 \\ \hline \end{array}$$
$$\begin{array}{r} 5 \\ -2 \\ \hline \end{array}$$

Name _____

Subtract.

3 − 2 =   7 − 5 =   8 − 1 =   4 − 1 =   9 − 9 =

5 − 3 =   6 − 5 =   7 − 7 =   8 − 5 =   6 − 3 =

9 − 5 =   6 − 4 =   7 − 1 =   8 − 4 =   9 − 1 =

8 − 0 =   5 − 1 =   6 − 3 =

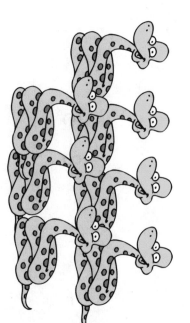

Subtraction

Subtract.

Name _____

$5 - 3 =$	$7 - 6 =$	$5 - 5 =$	$6 - 0 =$	$7 - 3 =$
$6 - 1 =$	$7 - 4 =$	$3 - 2 =$	$7 - 7 =$	$8 - 1 =$
$5 - 5 =$	$6 - 6 =$	$3 - 0 =$	$9 - 5 =$	$5 - 2 =$
$9 - 9 =$	$8 - 5 =$	$6 - 4 =$		

70

Name _____

Subtract.

6 − 4 =   8 − 5 =   6 − 6 =   4 − 4 =   3 − 1 =

4 − 0 =   4 − 3 =   8 − 8 =   7 − 6 =   8 − 0 =

3 − 0 =   6 − 4 =   8 − 0 =   5 − 4 =   4 − 2 =

1 − 1 =   2 − 2 =   8 − 3 =

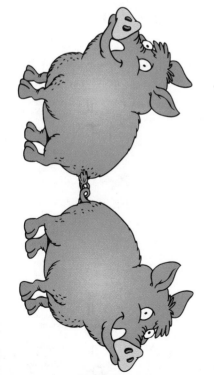

Subtraction

Name _____

Subtract.

$3 - 2 =$

$1 - 1 =$

$1 - 0 =$

$5 - 2 =$

$9 - 2 =$

$5 - 5 =$

$4 - 1 =$

$8 - 4 =$

$4 - 3 =$

$7 - 3 =$

$6 - 1 =$

$7 - 4 =$

$9 - 3 =$

$7 - 7 =$

$9 - 1 =$

$9 - 3 =$

$5 - 4 =$

$4 - 2 =$

72

Name _____

Subtraction	
☐	

Subtract.

7 − 7 =   4 − 3 =   8 − 7 =   5 − 5 =   3 − 1 =

7 − 2 =   9 − 0 =   6 − 4 =   6 − 6 =   5 − 1 =

3 − 3 =   7 − 7 =   8 − 5 =   4 − 4 =   1 − 0 =

5 − 2 =   7 − 5 =   5 − 3 =

73

Subtraction

Name _____

Subtract.

6 − 6 =   5 − 5 =   8 − 2 =   6 − 3 =

8 − 5 =   4 − 4 =   7 − 4 =   7 − 7 =

6 − 6 =   3 − 3 =   8 − 7 =   3 − 0 =

4 − 2 =   9 − 3 =   6 − 2 =   5 − 3 =

                                            3 − 2 =

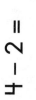

Name _____

Subtract.

3 − 2 =   8 − 5 =   4 − 3 =   9 − 0 =   6 − 6 =

$$\begin{array}{r} 4 \\ -4 \\ \hline \end{array}$$ $$\begin{array}{r} 6 \\ -3 \\ \hline \end{array}$$ $$\begin{array}{r} 8 \\ -7 \\ \hline \end{array}$$ $$\begin{array}{r} 6 \\ -1 \\ \hline \end{array}$$ $$\begin{array}{r} 4 \\ -0 \\ \hline \end{array}$$ $$\begin{array}{r} 7 \\ -3 \\ \hline \end{array}$$

5 − 5 =   3 − 3 =   7 − 6 =

Subtraction

Name _____

Subtract.

$6 - 2 =$

$4 - 3 =$

$6 - 3 =$

$8 - 8 =$

$9 - 5 =$

$$\begin{array}{r} 8 \\ -\ 0 \\ \hline \end{array}$$

$$\begin{array}{r} 4 \\ -\ 4 \\ \hline \end{array}$$

$$\begin{array}{r} 6 \\ -\ 1 \\ \hline \end{array}$$

$$\begin{array}{r} 7 \\ -\ 7 \\ \hline \end{array}$$

$$\begin{array}{r} 5 \\ -\ 3 \\ \hline \end{array}$$

$$\begin{array}{r} 8 \\ -\ 3 \\ \hline \end{array}$$

$3 - 2 =$

$1 - 1 =$

$7 - 6 =$

Name _____

Solve each problem.

Ken sees 8 birds.

3 fly away.

How many birds are left?

8
− 3
5

Carl sees 9 snails.

Tim takes 6 snails.

How many snails are left?

☐
− ☐
☐

Kathy has 8 ribbons.

She loses 7 ribbons.

How many ribbons are left?

Bob has 7 cards.

He gives 2 away.

How many cards are left?

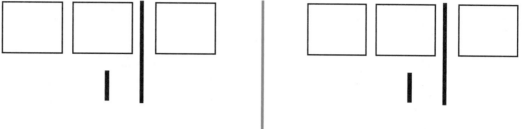
Solve each problem.

Tim has 9 kites.

He gives 7 away.

How many kites are left?

$\square$ $\square$ $-$ | $\square$

Sonny has 4 pencils.

1 pencil breaks.

How many pencils are left?

$\square$ $\square$ $-$ | $\square$

Dorthy has 8 shoes.

Her sister takes 2 shoes.

How many shoes are left?

$\square$ $\square$ $-$ | $\square$

Cliff draws 8 pictures.

He erases 7 pictures.

How many pictures are left?

$\square$ $\square$ $-$ | $\square$

Name _____

Solve each problem.

Doug sees 8 planes.

7 planes take off.

How many planes are left?

☐ − ☐ = ☐

Sam has 7 marbles.

He lost 4 at school.

How many marbles are left?

☐ − ☐ = ☐

Jen has 3 cakes.

Jon has 1 cake.

Jen has how many more cakes?

☐ − ☐ = ☐

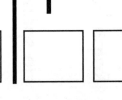

Ted has 5 bugs.

Chris has 3 bugs.

Ted has how many more bugs?

☐ − ☐ = ☐

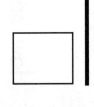

79

Subtraction Word Problems

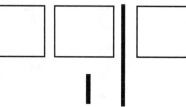

Subtraction

Solve each problem.

Name _____

Ben sees 7 cars.

4 cars drive away.

How many cars are left?

☐ − ☐ = ☐

Ralph has 8 dollars.

He spends 5 dollars.

How many dollars are left?

☐ − ☐ = ☐

Beth sees 9 leaves.

9 blow away.

How many leaves are left?

☐ − ☐ = ☐

Randy sees 6 boats.

3 boats leave.

How many boats are left?

☐ − ☐ = ☐

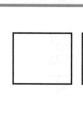

Name _____

Solve each problem.

George mows 5 lawns.

He finished 2 lawns.

How many lawns are left?

Dan's house is 9 miles away.

He has driven 8 miles.

How many miles are left?

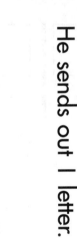

Devon can swim 9 laps.

She has swam 2 laps.

How many laps are left?

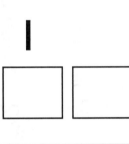

Luke writes 5 letters.

He sends out 1 letter.

How many letters are left?

  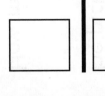

Subtraction Word Problems

Solve each problem.

Name _____

Lester sees 6 pennies.

He picks up 6 pennies.

How many pennies are left?

☐ − ☐ | ☐

Molly sees 8 cats.

2 cats run away.

How many cats are left?

☐ − ☐ | ☐

Al catches 7 fish.

Sam catches 4 fish.

Al has how many more fish?

☐ − ☐ | ☐

Jill has 3 presents.

She gives 2 away.

How many presents are left?

☐ − ☐ | ☐

Name _____

Subtract.

$$\begin{array}{r} 5\ 7 \\ -\quad 7 \\ \hline \end{array}\qquad \begin{array}{r} 1\ 5 \\ -\quad 6 \\ \hline \end{array}\qquad \begin{array}{r} 5\ 8 \\ -\quad 9 \\ \hline \end{array}\qquad \begin{array}{r} 9\ 8 \\ -\quad 2 \\ \hline \end{array}\qquad \begin{array}{r} 7\ 6 \\ -\quad 4 \\ \hline \end{array}\qquad \begin{array}{r} 4\ 2 \\ -\quad 1 \\ \hline \end{array}$$

$$\begin{array}{r} 4\ 5 \\ -\quad 7 \\ \hline \end{array}\qquad \begin{array}{r} 2\ 1 \\ -\quad 6 \\ \hline \end{array}\qquad \begin{array}{r} 6\ 5 \\ -\quad 3 \\ \hline \end{array}\qquad \begin{array}{r} 2\ 8 \\ -\quad 7 \\ \hline \end{array}\qquad \begin{array}{r} 4\ 6 \\ -\quad 8 \\ \hline \end{array}\qquad \begin{array}{r} 4\ 1 \\ -\quad 9 \\ \hline \end{array}$$

$$\begin{array}{r} 8\ 4 \\ -\quad 2 \\ \hline \end{array}\qquad \begin{array}{r} 7\ 6 \\ -\quad 3 \\ \hline \end{array}\qquad \begin{array}{r} 8\ 0 \\ -\quad 0 \\ \hline \end{array}\qquad \begin{array}{r} 3\ 1 \\ -\quad 9 \\ \hline \end{array}$$

Subtraction

Subtract.

Name

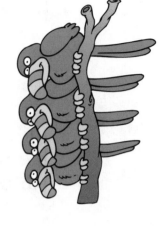

```
  5 8        8 4        1 0        4 3        5 4
  - 3        - 6        - 9        - 9        - 1
  ____       ____       ____       ____       ____

  3 2        6 4        5 3        6 8        7 7
  - 8        - 3        - 2        - 7        - 4
  ____       ____       ____       ____       ____

  3 1        1 1        8 5        3 3        9 0
  - 9        - 2        - 5        - 1        - 0
  ____       ____       ____       ____       ____

                                              7 5
                                              - 6
                                              ____
```

Name _____

Subtract.

$$\begin{array}{r} 6\ 4 \\ -\ \ 7 \\ \hline \end{array} \qquad \begin{array}{r} 5\ 6 \\ -\ \ 8 \\ \hline \end{array} \qquad \begin{array}{r} 9\ 9 \\ -\ \ 9 \\ \hline \end{array} \qquad \begin{array}{r} 7\ 4 \\ -\ \ 6 \\ \hline \end{array} \qquad \begin{array}{r} 8\ 5 \\ -\ \ 1 \\ \hline \end{array}$$

$$\begin{array}{r} 9\ 3 \\ -\ \ 5 \\ \hline \end{array} \qquad \begin{array}{r} 1\ 1 \\ -\ \ 1 \\ \hline \end{array} \qquad \begin{array}{r} 7\ 5 \\ -\ \ 4 \\ \hline \end{array} \qquad \begin{array}{r} 8\ 3 \\ -\ \ 1 \\ \hline \end{array} \qquad \begin{array}{r} 8\ 8 \\ -\ \ 4 \\ \hline \end{array}$$

$$\begin{array}{r} 1\ 4 \\ -\ \ 7 \\ \hline \end{array} \qquad \begin{array}{r} 9\ 5 \\ -\ \ 4 \\ \hline \end{array} \qquad \begin{array}{r} 7\ 4 \\ -\ \ 2 \\ \hline \end{array} \qquad \begin{array}{r} 3\ 2 \\ -\ \ 6 \\ \hline \end{array} \qquad \begin{array}{r} 4\ 3 \\ -\ \ 9 \\ \hline \end{array}$$

Subtract.

Name _____

Subtraction

$$\begin{array}{r}44\\-5\\\hline\end{array}$$

$$\begin{array}{r}86\\-5\\\hline\end{array}$$

$$\begin{array}{r}99\\-0\\\hline\end{array}$$

$$\begin{array}{r}85\\-6\\\hline\end{array}$$

$$\begin{array}{r}26\\-0\\\hline\end{array}$$

$$\begin{array}{r}42\\-6\\\hline\end{array}$$

$$\begin{array}{r}18\\-5\\\hline\end{array}$$

$$\begin{array}{r}28\\-7\\\hline\end{array}$$

$$\begin{array}{r}93\\-2\\\hline\end{array}$$

$$\begin{array}{r}67\\-2\\\hline\end{array}$$

$$\begin{array}{r}41\\-1\\\hline\end{array}$$

$$\begin{array}{r}74\\-2\\\hline\end{array}$$

$$\begin{array}{r}64\\-1\\\hline\end{array}$$

$$\begin{array}{r}65\\-4\\\hline\end{array}$$

$$\begin{array}{r}53\\-8\\\hline\end{array}$$

$$\begin{array}{r}55\\-5\\\hline\end{array}$$

Subtraction

Subtract.

Name ______________

63 − 2	74 − 8	24 − 8	65 − 4	55 − 3	65 − 2
46 − 7	87 − 2	75 − 9	49 − 2	51 − 6	44 − 7
51 − 3	64 − 1	73 − 7	10 − 4		

Subtract.

Name

$$\begin{array}{r} 37 \\ -\ 5 \\ \hline \end{array}$$

$$\begin{array}{r} 48 \\ -\ 2 \\ \hline \end{array}$$

$$\begin{array}{r} 95 \\ -\ 6 \\ \hline \end{array}$$

$$\begin{array}{r} 75 \\ -\ 4 \\ \hline \end{array}$$

$$\begin{array}{r} 55 \\ -\ 1 \\ \hline \end{array}$$

$$\begin{array}{r} 73 \\ -\ 7 \\ \hline \end{array}$$

$$\begin{array}{r} 32 \\ -\ 1 \\ \hline \end{array}$$

$$\begin{array}{r} 50 \\ -\ 0 \\ \hline \end{array}$$

$$\begin{array}{r} 42 \\ -\ 6 \\ \hline \end{array}$$

$$\begin{array}{r} 83 \\ -\ 9 \\ \hline \end{array}$$

$$\begin{array}{r} 19 \\ -\ 0 \\ \hline \end{array}$$

$$\begin{array}{r} 52 \\ -\ 7 \\ \hline \end{array}$$

$$\begin{array}{r} 31 \\ -\ 5 \\ \hline \end{array}$$

$$\begin{array}{r} 73 \\ -\ 1 \\ \hline \end{array}$$

$$\begin{array}{r} 53 \\ -\ 1 \\ \hline \end{array}$$

$$\begin{array}{r} 98 \\ -\ 2 \\ \hline \end{array}$$

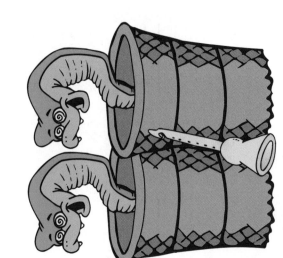

Name _____

Subtract.

74 – 2 =   95 – 3 =   44 – 1 =   99 – 0 =   85 – 3 =

84 – 1 =   59 – 4 =   51 – 3 =   48 – 1 =   68 – 9 =

39 – 5 =   73 – 2 =   59 – 9 =   62 – 8 =   77 – 3 =

56 – 8 =   59 – 0 =   75 – 1 =

Subtraction

Subtract.

Name _____

10 − 9 =	34 − 9 =	42 − 8 =
95 − 9 =	48 − 1 =	
48 − 2 =	76 − 1 =	45 − 0 =
59 − 3 =	84 − 8 =	
99 − 4 =	89 − 5 =	24 − 7 =
68 − 8 =	63 − 8 =	
74 − 8 =	74 − 0 =	
43 − 0 =		

Name _____

Subtract.

54 – 9 =   73 – 3 =   76 – 9 =   59 – 8 =   55 – 1 =

49 – 4 =   61 – 6 =   77 – 7 =   93 – 4 =   96 – 3 =

19 – 0 =   90 – 0 =   63 – 8 =   63 – 7 =   56 – 7 =

22 – 2 =   45 – 8 =   46 – 6 =

Subtraction

Name _____

Subtract.

95 − 7 =

10 − 5 =

74 − 8 =

21 − 0 =

21 − 4 =

83 − 0 =

63 − 1 =

92 − 9 =

73 − 1 =

65 − 7 =

60 − 1 =

36 − 9 =

64 − 7 =

74 − 3 =

52 − 1 =

89 − 0 =

Name _____

Subtract.

48 – 1 =

38 – 2 =

96 – 8 =

74 – 2 =

53 – 8 =

87 – 3 =

76 – 3 =

93 – 0 =

92 – 0 =

62 – 6 =

94 – 0 =

46 – 7 =

26 – 6 =

52 – 7 =

12 – 5 =

18 – 5 =

75 – 3 =

19 – 1 =

Subtraction

Name _____

Subtract.

47 − 1 =   37 − 8 =   32 − 1 =

46 − 8 =   73 − 6 =   45 − 9 =

73 − 0 =   85 − 3 =   84 − 8 =

                  12 − 9 =   43 − 3 =

10 − 9 =   55 − 8 =   99 − 9 =   33 − 7 =

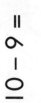

Name _____

Subtract.

87 − 1 =   12 − 9 =   24 − 7 =   62 − 0 =   48 − 7 =

$$\begin{array}{r} 3\ 6 \\ -\ \ 2 \\ \hline \end{array}$$
$$\begin{array}{r} 1\ 9 \\ -\ \ 5 \\ \hline \end{array}$$
$$\begin{array}{r} 4\ 2 \\ -\ \ 9 \\ \hline \end{array}$$
$$\begin{array}{r} 6\ 4 \\ -\ \ 3 \\ \hline \end{array}$$
$$\begin{array}{r} 7\ 4 \\ -\ \ 4 \\ \hline \end{array}$$
$$\begin{array}{r} 8\ 3 \\ -\ \ 0 \\ \hline \end{array}$$

35 − 1 =   74 − 5 =   95 − 1 =

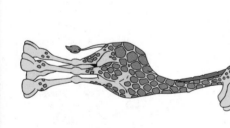

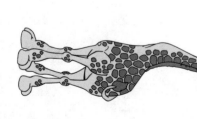

Subtract.

Name _____

$53 - 4 =$

$72 - 8 =$

$38 - 7 =$

$66 - 0 =$

$73 - 0 =$

$$\begin{array}{r} 5\ 3 \\ -\ 9 \\ \hline \end{array}$$

$$\begin{array}{r} 4\ 5 \\ -\ 0 \\ \hline \end{array}$$

$$\begin{array}{r} 1\ 8 \\ -\ 6 \\ \hline \end{array}$$

$$\begin{array}{r} 4\ 3 \\ -\ 1 \\ \hline \end{array}$$

$$\begin{array}{r} 9\ 5 \\ -\ 9 \\ \hline \end{array}$$

$$\begin{array}{r} 7\ 6 \\ -\ 3 \\ \hline \end{array}$$

$74 - 4 =$

$63 - 1 =$

$63 - 8 =$

Subtraction Word Problems

Solve each problem.

Ken sees 25 birds.

8 flew away.

How many birds are left?

$$
\begin{array}{r}
2\,5 \\
-\ \ 8 \\
\hline
1\,7
\end{array}
$$

Doug has 73 books.

He gives 9 away.

How many books are left?

$$
\begin{array}{r}
\,\cancel{7}\,3 \\
-\ \ 9 \\
\hline
\,4
\end{array}
$$

Tom delivers 76 papers.

He delivered 8 papers.

How many are left?

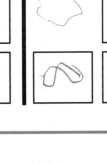

$$
\begin{array}{r}
7\,6 \\
-\ \ 8 \\
\hline
6\,8
\end{array}
$$

Tammy has 52 mints.

She eats 2 mints.

How many mints are left?

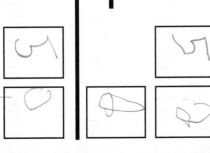

$$
\begin{array}{r}
5\,2 \\
-\ \ 2 \\
\hline
5\,0
\end{array}
$$

Subtraction Word Problems

Solve each problem.

Name _____

Amy baked 58 cookies.

Dan eats 6 cookies.

How many are left?

Lindsay has 87 tickets.

She sold 9 tickets.

How many tickets are left?

Pam sees 14 dogs.

9 dogs run away.

How many dogs are left?

Don rented 10 movies.

He returned 5 movies.

How many movies are left?

Name _____

Solve each problem.

Margie has 18 balloons.

9 balloons fly away.

How many balloons are left?

Ruth sees 45 cars.

1 car drives away.

How many cars are left?

John has 34 pens.

He lost 4 pens.

How many pens are left?

Ken sees 25 birds.

8 birds fly away.

How many birds are left?

Subtraction Word Problems

Solve each problem.

Name _____

Emily sees 21 flies.

6 flies fly away.

How many flies are left?

$$\begin{array}{c}\square\square \\ \hline - \\ \hline \square\square \end{array}$$

Erin has 10 watches.

3 watches break.

How many watches are left?

$$\begin{array}{c}\square\square \\ - \\ \hline \square\square \end{array}$$

Dave sees 63 clouds.

3 clouds drift away.

How many clouds are left?

$$\begin{array}{c}\square\square \\ - \\ \hline \square\square \end{array}$$

Corey has 57 cards.

He keeps them all.

How many cards are left?

$$\begin{array}{c}\square\square \\ - \\ \hline \square\square \end{array}$$

Name _____

Solve each problem.

Randy has 10 bikes.

He gives 5 to his friends.

How many bikes are left?

[ ] [ ]
—
[ ] [ ]

Fred has 35 peas.

He eats 9 peas.

How many peas are left?

[ ] [ ]
—
[ ] [ ]

Donna has 74 dollars.

She spends 6 dollars.

How many dollars are left?

[ ] [ ]
[ ]
—
[ ] [ ]

Brenda sees 35 planes.

7 planes take off.

How many planes are left?

[ ] [ ]
[ ]
—
[ ] [ ]

Subtraction

Solve each problem.

Name _____

Ben has 84 toys.

He gives 6 away.

☐☐ ☐
—
☐

How many toys are left?

Andy orders 10 pizzas.

4 pizzas arrive.

☐☐ ☐
—
☐

How many pizzas are missing?

Tammy has 39 dolls.

She gives 1 away.

☐☐ ☐☐
—
☐☐

How many dolls are left?

Amy has 14 earrings.

She loses 2 earrings.

☐☐ ☐☐
—
☐☐

How many earrings are left?

Name _____

Subtract.

```
  6 3        5 9        3 5        4 1        4 5
- 5 1      - 5 0      - 2 2      - 3 0      - 3 2
```

```
  6 5        4 1        9 0        1 0        7 3
- 6 2      - 3 3      - 3 4      - 1 0      - 5 8
```

```
  7 8        6 5        5 5        6 3        2 0
- 3 9      - 3 7      - 5 2      - 4 7      - 1 9
```

Subtraction

Subtract.

Name _____

68 − 4 5	67 − 4 3	76 − 5 0	55 − 4 9	74 − 5 2
83 − 3 6	62 − 3 2	41 − 2 7	51 − 3 5	19 − 1 8
97 − 9 0	45 − 3 1	94 − 6 3	64 − 6 2	38 − 2 5

Name _____

Subtract.

$$\begin{array}{r} 7\,2 \\ -\,3\,6 \\ \hline \end{array}$$
$$\begin{array}{r} 4\,2 \\ -\,3\,6 \\ \hline \end{array}$$
$$\begin{array}{r} 8\,3 \\ -\,5\,7 \\ \hline \end{array}$$
$$\begin{array}{r} 9\,4 \\ -\,6\,8 \\ \hline \end{array}$$
$$\begin{array}{r} 6\,4 \\ -\,6\,1 \\ \hline \end{array}$$
$$\begin{array}{r} 9\,3 \\ -\,6\,7 \\ \hline \end{array}$$

$$\begin{array}{r} 8\,9 \\ -\,1\,0 \\ \hline \end{array}$$
$$\begin{array}{r} 8\,2 \\ -\,3\,7 \\ \hline \end{array}$$
$$\begin{array}{r} 9\,9 \\ -\,8\,2 \\ \hline \end{array}$$
$$\begin{array}{r} 9\,5 \\ -\,9\,5 \\ \hline \end{array}$$
$$\begin{array}{r} 6\,5 \\ -\,4\,2 \\ \hline \end{array}$$
$$\begin{array}{r} 5\,8 \\ -\,3\,7 \\ \hline \end{array}$$

$$\begin{array}{r} 5\,2 \\ -\,3\,8 \\ \hline \end{array}$$
$$\begin{array}{r} 6\,6 \\ -\,2\,4 \\ \hline \end{array}$$
$$\begin{array}{r} 6\,3 \\ -\,5\,1 \\ \hline \end{array}$$
$$\begin{array}{r} 4\,1 \\ -\,3\,7 \\ \hline \end{array}$$

Subtraction

Name _____

Subtract.

$$
\begin{array}{r}
8\ 2 \\
-\ 4\ 1 \\
\hline
\end{array}
\qquad
\begin{array}{r}
8\ 1 \\
-\ 4\ 7 \\
\hline
\end{array}
\qquad
\begin{array}{r}
5\ 2 \\
-\ 3\ 1 \\
\hline
\end{array}
\qquad
\begin{array}{r}
7\ 4 \\
-\ 2\ 6 \\
\hline
\end{array}
\qquad
\begin{array}{r}
8\ 6 \\
-\ 4\ 4 \\
\hline
\end{array}
\qquad
\begin{array}{r}
6\ 7 \\
-\ 4\ 5 \\
\hline
\end{array}
$$

$$
\begin{array}{r}
5\ 1 \\
-\ 1\ 9 \\
\hline
\end{array}
\qquad
\begin{array}{r}
6\ 2 \\
-\ 4\ 7 \\
\hline
\end{array}
\qquad
\begin{array}{r}
7\ 2 \\
-\ 4\ 6 \\
\hline
\end{array}
\qquad
\begin{array}{r}
4\ 1 \\
-\ 3\ 8 \\
\hline
\end{array}
\qquad
\begin{array}{r}
7\ 6 \\
-\ 2\ 1 \\
\hline
\end{array}
\qquad
\begin{array}{r}
4\ 2 \\
-\ 3\ 8 \\
\hline
\end{array}
$$

$$
\begin{array}{r}
8\ 8 \\
-\ 4\ 2 \\
\hline
\end{array}
\qquad
\begin{array}{r}
2\ 0 \\
-\ 1\ 9 \\
\hline
\end{array}
\qquad
\begin{array}{r}
7\ 3 \\
-\ 5\ 8 \\
\hline
\end{array}
\qquad
\begin{array}{r}
7\ 5 \\
-\ 5\ 8 \\
\hline
\end{array}
$$

106

Name _____

Subtraction

Subtract.

```
  8 3        8 9        7 3        9 1        7 2        8 3
- 5 5      - 4 5      - 4 8      - 4 0      - 5 1      - 5 8
_____     _____     _____     _____     _____     _____


  9 6        9 8        8 2        5 5        8 3        9 2
- 4 7      - 2 6      - 3 7      - 5 2      - 5 7      - 5 7
_____     _____     _____     _____     _____     _____


  6 2        5 7        6 1        3 5
- 4 9      - 2 2      - 3 5      - 2 7
_____     _____     _____     _____
```

Subtraction

Name _____

Subtract.

1 8 − 1 3	4 6 − 4 2	4 1 − 3 6

6 2 − 3 6	6 2 − 4 1	7 5 − 5 3

8 3 − 5 6	1 5 − 1 2	7 5 − 4 6

7 4 − 5 8	6 8 − 4 9	6 2 − 4 7

5 5 − 3 8	8 5 − 3 3	6 3 − 4 8

6 4 − 2 1	

Name _____

Subtract.

61 – 22 =   63 – 10 =   11 – 11 =   60 – 37 =   73 – 33 =

73 – 36 =   74 – 29 =   35 – 21 =   34 – 10 =   63 – 14 =

51 – 24 =   94 – 87 =   63 – 29 =   99 – 98 =   37 – 25 =

84 – 47 =   58 – 11 =   84 – 63 =

Subraction

Name _____

Subtract.

49 − 30 =

66 − 23 =

14 − 12 =

16 − 10 =

86 − 75 =

75 − 67 =

52 − 29 =

53 − 51 =

53 − 42 =

56 − 31 =

96 − 84 =

84 − 75 =

62 − 23 =

61 − 13 =

64 − 61 =

52 − 13 =

96 − 75 =

89 − 71 =

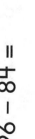

110

Name _____

Subtract.

16 – 14 =   46 – 37 =   91 – 88 =   65 – 61 =

61 – 37 =   95 – 61 =   60 – 51 =   79 – 64 =   49 – 13 =

18 – 10 =   64 – 62 =   76 – 71 =   16 – 11 =   94 – 76 =

49 – 43 =   77 – 26 =   65 – 59 =

Subtraction

Subtract.

Name _____

Subtraction

$$61 - 24 =$$

$$63 - 57 =$$

$$46 - 26 =$$

$$51 - 32 =$$

$$68 - 59 =$$

$$94 - 86 =$$

$$68 - 61 =$$

$$99 - 99 =$$

$$48 - 39 =$$

$$63 - 41 =$$

$$97 - 10 =$$

$$63 - 29 =$$

$$84 - 67 =$$

$$16 - 12 =$$

$$98 - 76 =$$

$$54 - 28 =$$

$$98 - 39 =$$

$$82 - 68 =$$

Subtraction

Name _____

Subtract.

84 – 76 =   67 – 43 =   16 – 14 =   49 – 24 =   55 – 11 =

62 – 28 =   69 – 51 =   59 – 24 =   94 – 37 =   62 – 28 =

45 – 43 =   57 – 20 =   26 – 23 =   67 – 29 =   92 – 24 =

92 – 11 =   43 – 29 =   19 – 10 =

113

Subtraction

Name _____

Subtract.

76 − 26 =	94 − 68 =	42 − 37 =
	49 − 43 =	
19 − 13 =	49 − 48 =	55 − 24 =
	57 − 52 =	89 − 49 =
67 − 59 =	16 − 10 =	92 − 46 =
	29 − 25 =	
56 − 28 =	10 − 10 =	47 − 19 =

49 − 43 =

Name _____

Subtract.

59 – 46 =   94 – 23 =   61 – 28 =   91 – 18 =   76 – 20 =

$$\begin{array}{r} 5\,8 \\ -\ 2\,4 \\ \hline \end{array} \qquad \begin{array}{r} 8\,3 \\ -\ 3\,0 \\ \hline \end{array} \qquad \begin{array}{r} 6\,5 \\ -\ 6\,2 \\ \hline \end{array} \qquad \begin{array}{r} 7\,9 \\ -\ 5\,6 \\ \hline \end{array} \qquad \begin{array}{r} 2\,0 \\ -\ 1\,9 \\ \hline \end{array} \qquad \begin{array}{r} 3\,8 \\ -\ 1\,7 \\ \hline \end{array}$$

57 – 29 =   46 – 37 =   90 – 80 =

Subtraction

Name _____

Subtract.

67 − 24 =

49 − 37 =

49 − 48 =

93 − 10 =

52 − 47 =

$$\begin{array}{r} 6\ 5 \\ -\ 4\ 8 \\ \hline \end{array}$$

$$\begin{array}{r} 2\ 5 \\ -\ 2\ 2 \\ \hline \end{array}$$

$$\begin{array}{r} 6\ 3 \\ -\ 4\ 1 \\ \hline \end{array}$$

$$\begin{array}{r} 7\ 8 \\ -\ 4\ 3 \\ \hline \end{array}$$

$$\begin{array}{r} 9\ 7 \\ -\ 9\ 5 \\ \hline \end{array}$$

$$\begin{array}{r} 1\ 1 \\ -\ 1\ 1 \\ \hline \end{array}$$

67 − 15 =

46 − 28 =

79 − 29 =

116

Name _____

Solve each problem.

Ken sees 25 birds.

20 birds flew away.

How many birds are left?

$$
\begin{array}{r}
2\;5 \\
-\;2\;0 \\
\hline
\;5
\end{array}
$$

Roger has 74 marbles.

Steve takes 49 marbles.

How many marbles are left?

$$
\begin{array}{r}
\Box\;\Box \\
-\;\Box\;\Box \\
\hline
\Box\;\Box
\end{array}
$$

Bob has 48 toys.

He gives them all away.

How many toys are left?

$$
\begin{array}{r}
\Box\;\Box \\
-\;\Box\;\Box \\
\hline
\Box\;\Box
\end{array}
$$

Molly sees 83 cars.

37 cars drive away.

How many cars are left?

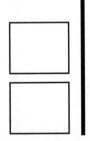

$$
\begin{array}{r}
\Box\;\Box \\
-\;\Box\;\Box \\
\hline
\Box\;\Box
\end{array}
$$

Subtraction Word Problems

Solve each problem.

Name _____

Doug has 89 dollars.

He spends 72 dollars.

How many dollars are left?

$$\begin{array}{c} \square\ \square \\[2pt] \square\ \square \end{array}\ -\ \begin{array}{c} \square \\[2pt] \square \end{array}$$

The pond has 64 fish.

Stacey catches 24 fish.

How many fish are left?

$$\begin{array}{c} \square\ \square \\[2pt] \square\ \square \end{array}\ -\ \begin{array}{c} \square \\[2pt] \square \end{array}$$

Cliff draws 74 squares.

He erases 38 squares.

How many squares are left?

$$\begin{array}{c} \square\ \square \\[2pt] \square\ \square \end{array}\ -\ \begin{array}{c} \square \\[2pt] \square \end{array}$$

Jen bakes 24 cakes.

She gives 19 to friends.

How many cakes are left?

$$\begin{array}{c} \square\ \square \\[2pt] \square\ \square \end{array}\ -\ \begin{array}{c} \square \end{array}$$

Solve each problem.

Name _____

Roger sees 68 bugs.

52 bugs crawl away.

How many bugs are left?

Luke writes 93 letters.

He sends out 74 letters.

How many letters are left?

Jill's house is 78 miles away.

She has gone 63 miles.

How many miles are left?

Al delivers 24 papers.

He delivered 10.

How many papers are left?

Subtraction Word Problems

Name _____

Solve each problem.

Rebecca has 87 marbles.

She loses 33 marbles.

How many marbles are left?

Blake sees 69 bees.

12 bees fly away.

How many bees are left?

Doug has 59 books.

He gives 32 away.

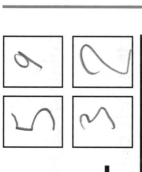

books

How many books are left?

Robert sees 70 leaves.

68 leaves blow away.

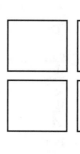

How many leaves are left?

Name _____

Solve each problem.

Al and Tim play 24 games.

Al wins 17 games.

How many did Tim win?

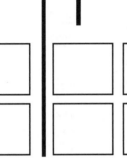

Jen sees 74 boxes.

62 boxes get moved.

How many boxes are left?

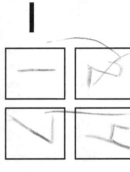

Kevin has 48 pens.

He loses 12.

How many pens are left?

Ralph sees 37 ants.

18 ants go in the anthill.

How many ants are left?

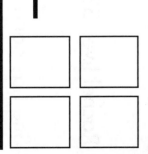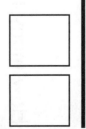

Subtraction Word Problems

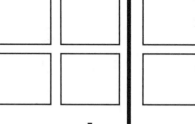

Solve each problem.

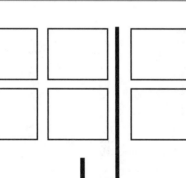

There are 59 trucks.

48 trucks drive away.

How many trucks are left?

Bob can run 26 miles.

He runs 12 miles.

How many miles are left?

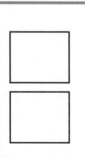

Rachel lives 38 miles away.

She has gone 38 miles.

How many miles are left?

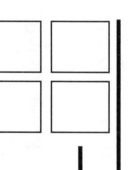

Ted has 62 balloons.

39 balloons fly away.

How many balloons are left?

Page 3
7 4 10 5 15 11
10 9 7 3 9 9
12 9 15 10

Page 4
3 11 8 10 1
12 17 12 12 13 11
10 14 2 8

Page 5
10 18 12 8 4 0
14 12 6 12 13
13 6 3 11

Page 6
9 0 5 6 16 14
11 9 8 16 10 6
10 15 14 13

Page 7
9 14 17 7 13 4
2 10 13 8 9 14
12 5 10 9

Page 8
7 6 16 8 10 7
10 14 8 3 17 11
7 12 11 5

Page 9
14 4 17 5 13
2 9 10 8 12
14 0 12

Page 10
8 4 8 8 11
6 3 12 14 9
12 15 11 12
9 8 17

Page 11
13 4 16 12
6 14 7 11 6
9 16 9 8 0
9 11 11

Page 12
13 3 5 17 9
10 8 16 8 11
7 11 11 9 3
14 6 11

Page 13
6 10 6 4 13
8 12 10 9 11
13 13 7 11 10
12 12 14

Page 14
7 9 15 12 7
6 12 10 15 13
15 5 3 3 12
11 13 12

Page 15
6 14 12 9 7
14 12 0 6 13 9
13 2 9

Page 16
11 18 8 4 8
6 16 8 15 6 15
9 8 7

Page 17

$$\begin{array}{r}2\\+3\\\hline5\end{array}\qquad\begin{array}{r}3\\+8\\\hline11\end{array}\qquad\begin{array}{r}1\\+2\\\hline3\end{array}\qquad\begin{array}{r}7\\+9\\\hline16\end{array}$$

Page 18

$$\begin{array}{r}5\\+9\\\hline14\end{array}\qquad\begin{array}{r}2\\+5\\\hline7\end{array}\qquad\begin{array}{r}8\\+7\\\hline15\end{array}\qquad\begin{array}{r}4\\+2\\\hline6\end{array}$$

Page 19

$$\begin{array}{r}5\\+0\\\hline5\end{array}\qquad\begin{array}{r}2\\+1\\\hline3\end{array}\qquad\begin{array}{r}9\\+9\\\hline18\end{array}\qquad\begin{array}{r}3\\+7\\\hline10\end{array}$$

Page 20

$$\begin{array}{r}6\\+3\\\hline4\end{array}\qquad\begin{array}{r}8\\+8\\\hline14\end{array}\qquad\begin{array}{r}3\\+5\\\hline13\end{array}\qquad\begin{array}{r}+8\\\hline11\end{array}$$

Page 21

$$\begin{array}{r}2\\+7\\\hline9\end{array}\qquad\begin{array}{r}1\\+2\\\hline3\end{array}\qquad\begin{array}{r}5\\+8\\\hline13\end{array}\qquad\begin{array}{r}3\\+9\\\hline12\end{array}$$

Page 22

$$\begin{array}{r}2\\+3\\\hline5\end{array}\qquad\begin{array}{r}2\\+9\\\hline11\end{array}\qquad\begin{array}{r}6\\+4\\\hline10\end{array}\qquad\begin{array}{r}5\\+3\\\hline8\end{array}$$

Page 23
47 21 93 95 28 78
38 104 42 26 20 99
74 41 52 43

Page 24
20 52 98 99 34 80
40 71 50 28 13 47
87 49 35 42

Page 25
77 22 89 89 29 88
55 30 32 46 49 37
13 69 69 91

Page 26
37 81 32 101 43 43
46 15 48 35 97 84
25 71 98 61

Page 27
59 55 12 60 53 52
71 27 76 22 32 89
17 44 23 84

Page 28
31 29 99 52 23 45
70 59 54 42 31 28
14 24 27 81

Page 29
36 22 56 73 20
28 102 85 36 79
85 69 98 50
55 88 58

Page 30
72 21 93 26 93
64 65 75 100 76
35 12 89 48 97
74 42 21

Page 31
33 85 72 92 25
52 47 18 73 50
49 22 77 95 97
81 25 88

Page 32
86 74 34 84 70
60 22 33 58 23
98 14 39 100 41
42 56 74

Page 33
65 89 67 69 39
97 39 35 76 54
64 28 63 52 67
38 61 91

Page 34
97 98 65 89 58
70 70 34 96 67
38 82 43 69 98
13 41 24

Page 35
16 99 80 54 71
57 33 94 50 49 15
90 14 44

Page 36
95 70 40 41 91
71 45 84 49 68 42
44 61 95

Page 37

$$\begin{array}{r}25\\+8\\\hline33\end{array}\qquad\begin{array}{r}37\\+8\\\hline45\end{array}\qquad\begin{array}{r}87\\+0\\\hline87\end{array}\qquad\begin{array}{r}66\\+7\\\hline73\end{array}$$

Page 38

$$\begin{array}{r}12\\+8\\\hline20\end{array}\qquad\begin{array}{r}22\\+7\\\hline29\end{array}\qquad\begin{array}{r}48\\+5\\\hline53\end{array}\qquad\begin{array}{r}14\\+6\\\hline20\end{array}$$

Page 39

$$\begin{array}{r}11\\+2\\\hline13\end{array}\qquad\begin{array}{r}62\\+1\\\hline63\end{array}\qquad\begin{array}{r}12\\+9\\\hline21\end{array}\qquad\begin{array}{r}74\\+9\\\hline83\end{array}$$

Page 40

$$\begin{array}{r}11\\+1\\\hline12\end{array}\qquad\begin{array}{r}24\\+8\\\hline32\end{array}\qquad\begin{array}{r}47\\+4\\\hline51\end{array}\qquad\begin{array}{r}35\\+7\\\hline42\end{array}$$

Page 41

$$\begin{array}{r}14\\+8\\\hline22\end{array}\qquad\begin{array}{r}11\\+2\\\hline13\end{array}\qquad\begin{array}{r}46\\+5\\\hline51\end{array}\qquad\begin{array}{r}83\\+3\\\hline86\end{array}$$

Page 42

$$\begin{array}{r}20\\+7\\\hline27\end{array}\qquad\begin{array}{r}25\\+8\\\hline33\end{array}\qquad\begin{array}{r}48\\+3\\\hline51\end{array}\qquad\begin{array}{r}11\\+4\\\hline15\end{array}$$

Page 43
92	111	34	159
103	65	113	90
169	70	110	83

Page 44
66	119	48	61	39	117
131	78	140	102	117	120
52	115	117	41		

Page 45
136	113	100	107	60	110
130	144	80	53	112	121
91	183	131	85		

Page 46
62	103	63	49	48	46
131	107	109	130	126	125
129	140	92	123		

Page 47
105	104	75	110	121	79
164	97	79	97	120	99
52	121	129	81		

Page 48
112	90	184	87	105	125
116	130	152	142	107	57
52	98	101	143		

Page 49
110	122	105	157	24
93	125	158	101	147
64	150	113	85	130
68	179	93		

Page 50
139	129	81	190	141
62	97	28	86	142
127	43	109	108	101
131	22	53		

Page 51
75	87	43	95	94
93	81	110	55	134
128	91	34	124	80
90	95	157		

Page 52
146	128	74	157	109
103	41	170	148	59
115	72	118	59	144
63	55	157		

Page 53
39	133	174	127	89
121	98	114	113	143
83	133	134	72	132
123	103	38		

Page 54
110	146	109	154	113
42	124	69	144	155
110	132	155	64	147
95	91	99		

Page 55
97	104	110	151	74	
105	77	102	126	55	88
91	118	72			

Page 56
144	25	155	87	74	
170	126	142	146	112	128
90	126	72			

Page 57

$$\begin{array}{r} 25 \\ +20 \\ \hline 45 \end{array} \qquad \begin{array}{r} 88 \\ +75 \\ \hline 163 \end{array} \qquad \begin{array}{r} 11 \\ +25 \\ \hline 36 \end{array} \qquad \begin{array}{r} 53 \\ +87 \\ \hline 140 \end{array}$$

Page 58

$$\begin{array}{r} 78 \\ +64 \\ \hline 142 \end{array} \qquad \begin{array}{r} 11 \\ +37 \\ \hline 48 \end{array} \qquad \begin{array}{r} 38 \\ +91 \\ \hline 129 \end{array} \qquad \begin{array}{r} 48 \\ +62 \\ \hline 110 \end{array}$$

Page 59

$$\begin{array}{r} 38 \\ +61 \\ \hline 99 \end{array} \qquad \begin{array}{r} 10 \\ +12 \\ \hline 22 \end{array} \qquad \begin{array}{r} 29 \\ +48 \\ \hline 77 \end{array} \qquad \begin{array}{r} 73 \\ +48 \\ \hline 121 \end{array}$$

Page 60

$$\begin{array}{r} 39 \\ +27 \\ \hline 66 \end{array} \qquad \begin{array}{r} 36 \\ +72 \\ \hline 108 \end{array} \qquad \begin{array}{r} 10 \\ +13 \\ \hline 23 \end{array} \qquad \begin{array}{r} 31 \\ +48 \\ \hline 79 \end{array}$$

Page 61

$$\begin{array}{r} 20 \\ +52 \\ \hline 72 \end{array} \qquad \begin{array}{r} 73 \\ +35 \\ \hline 108 \end{array} \qquad \begin{array}{r} 14 \\ +36 \\ \hline 50 \end{array} \qquad \begin{array}{r} 10 \\ +39 \\ \hline 49 \end{array}$$

Page 62

$$\begin{array}{r} 29 \\ +52 \\ \hline 81 \end{array} \qquad \begin{array}{r} 86 \\ +65 \\ \hline 151 \end{array} \qquad \begin{array}{r} 38 \\ +63 \\ \hline 101 \end{array} \qquad \begin{array}{r} 73 \\ +10 \\ \hline 83 \end{array}$$

Page 63
0 4 7 1 3
4 0 7 3 0 5
0 2 4 3

Page 64
0 5 2 9 0 2
3 8 5 1 1 0
3 0 4 6

Page 65
0 2 4 2 4 6
4 3 8 3 0 4
3 5 2 2

Page 66
3 1 1 7 0 6
6 5 3 1 0 0
4 1 3 5

Page 67
2 5 0 3 2 4
0 0 3 0 3 0
0 1 7 3

Page 68
2 2 4 0 1 3
0 0 7 0 4 3
3 3 0 0

Page 69
1 2 7 3 0
2 1 0 3 3
4 2 6 4 8
8 4 3

Page 70
2 1 0 6 4
5 3 1 0 7
0 0 3 4 3
0 3 2

Page 71
2 3 0 0 2
4 1 0 1 8
3 2 8 1 2
0 0 5

Page 72
1 0 1 3 7
0 3 4 1 4
5 3 6 0 8
6 1 2

Page 73
0 1 1 0 2
5 9 2 0 4
0 0 3 0 1
3 2 2

Page 74
0 0 6 6 3
3 0 3 3 0
0 0 1 2 1
2 6 4

Page 75
1 3 1 9 0
0 3 1 5 4 4
0 0 1

Page 76
4 1 3 0 4
8 0 5 0 2 5
1 0 1

Page 77

$$8 - 3 = 5 \quad 9 - 6 = 3 \quad 8 - 7 = 1 \quad 7 - 2 = 5$$

Page 78

$$9 - 7 = 2 \quad 4 - 1 = 3 \quad 8 - 2 = 6 \quad 8 - 7 = 1$$

Page 79

$$8 - 7 = 1 \quad 7 - 4 = 3 \quad 3 - 1 = 2 \quad 5 - 3 = 2$$

Page 80

$$7 - 4 = 3 \quad 9 - 9 = 0 \quad 8 - 5 = 3 \quad 6 - 3 = 3$$

Page 81

$$5 - 2 = 3 \quad 9 - 2 = 7 \quad 9 - 8 = 1 \quad 5 - 1 = 4$$

Page 82

$$6 - 6 = 0 \quad 8 - 2 = 6 \quad 7 - 4 = 3 \quad 3 - 2 = 1$$

Page 83
50 9 49 96 72 41
38 15 62 21 38 32
82 73 80 22

Page 84
55 78 1 34 73 53
24 61 51 61 90 69
22 9 80 32

Page 85
57 48 90 12 68 84
88 10 71 82 84 34
7 91 72 26

Page 86
39 81 99 79 26 36
13 21 91 65 40 72
63 61 45 50

Page 87
61 66 16 61 52 63
39 85 66 47 45 37
48 63 66 6

Page 88
32 46 89 71 74 54
66 31 50 36 52 96
19 45 26 72

Page 89
72 92 43 99 82
83 55 48 47 59
34 71 50 54 74
48 59 74

Page 90
1 86 25 47 34
46 56 75 76 45
95 60 84 55 17
66 43 74

Page 91
45 70 67 51 54
45 55 70 89 93
19 90 55 56 49
20 37 40

Page 92
88 89 5 66 21
17 83 36 62 83
72 58 59 27 57
71 51 89

Page 93
47 36 88 72 45
84 73 93 92 56
94 39 20 45 7
13 72 18

Page 94
46 35 29 72 31
38 67 32 76 36
73 82 3 40 26
1 90 47

Page 95
86 3 17 62 41
34 14 33 61 70 83
34 69 94

Page 96
49 64 31 66 73
44 45 12 42 86 73
70 62 55

Page 97

$$
\begin{array}{rrrr}
25 & 73 & 76 & 52 \\
-8 & -9 & -8 & -2 \\
\hline
17 & 64 & 68 & 50
\end{array}
$$

Page 98

$$
\begin{array}{rrrr}
58 & 14 & 87 & 10 \\
-6 & -9 & -9 & -5 \\
\hline
52 & 5 & 68 & 5
\end{array}
$$

Page 99

$$
\begin{array}{rrrr}
18 & 45 & 34 & 25 \\
-9 & -1 & -4 & -8 \\
\hline
9 & 44 & 30 & 17
\end{array}
$$

Page 100

$$
\begin{array}{rrrr}
21 & 10 & 63 & 57 \\
-6 & -3 & -3 & -0 \\
\hline
15 & 7 & 60 & 57
\end{array}
$$

Page 101

$$
\begin{array}{rrrr}
10 & 35 & 74 & 35 \\
-5 & -9 & -6 & -7 \\
\hline
5 & 26 & 68 & 28
\end{array}
$$

Page 102

$$
\begin{array}{rrrr}
84 & 39 & 10 & 14 \\
-6 & -1 & -4 & -2 \\
\hline
78 & 38 & 6 & 12
\end{array}
$$

Answer Key

Page 103
12 9 13 11 41 13
3 8 56 0 15 1
39 28 3 16

Page 104
23 24 26 6 1 22
47 30 14 16 13 24
7 14 31 2

Page 105
36 6 26 26 3 26
79 45 17 0 23 21
14 42 12 4

Page 106
22 42 48 21 34 41
4 55 3 26 15 32
77 15 1 46

Page 107
28 44 25 51 21 25
49 72 45 3 26 35
13 35 26 8

Page 108
17 16 27 5 4 5
52 19 3 22 21 26
43 15 15 29

Page 109
39 53 0 23 40
37 45 14 24 49
27 7 34 1 12
37 47 21

Page 110
19 43 2 6 11
8 23 2 11 25
12 9 39 48 3
39 21 18

Page 111
2 9 20 3 4
24 34 9 15 36
8 2 5 5 18
6 51 6

Page 112
37 6 20 19 9
8 7 0 9 22
87 34 17 4 22
26 59 14

Page 113
8 24 2 25 44
34 18 35 57 34
2 37 3 38 68
81 14 9

Page 114
50 26 6 5 5
6 1 5 40 31
8 6 4 15 46
28 0 68

Page 115
13 71 33 73 56
34 53 3 23 1 21
28 9 10

Page 116
43 12 1 83 5
17 3 22 35 2 0
52 18 50

Page 117

$$
\begin{array}{r} 25 \\ -20 \\ \hline 5 \end{array} \quad
\begin{array}{r} 74 \\ -49 \\ \hline 25 \end{array} \quad
\begin{array}{r} 48 \\ -48 \\ \hline 0 \end{array} \quad
\begin{array}{r} 83 \\ -37 \\ \hline 46 \end{array}
$$

Page 118

$$
\begin{array}{r} 89 \\ -72 \\ \hline 17 \end{array} \quad
\begin{array}{r} 64 \\ -24 \\ \hline 40 \end{array} \quad
\begin{array}{r} 74 \\ -38 \\ \hline 36 \end{array} \quad
\begin{array}{r} 24 \\ -19 \\ \hline 5 \end{array}
$$

Page 119

$$
\begin{array}{r} 68 \\ -52 \\ \hline 16 \end{array} \quad
\begin{array}{r} 93 \\ -74 \\ \hline 19 \end{array} \quad
\begin{array}{r} 78 \\ -63 \\ \hline 15 \end{array} \quad
\begin{array}{r} 24 \\ -10 \\ \hline 14 \end{array}
$$

Page 120

$$
\begin{array}{r} 59 \\ -32 \\ \hline 27 \end{array} \quad
\begin{array}{r} 87 \\ -33 \\ \hline 54 \end{array} \quad
\begin{array}{r} 70 \\ -68 \\ \hline 2 \end{array} \quad
\begin{array}{r} 69 \\ -12 \\ \hline 57 \end{array}
$$

Page 121

$$
\begin{array}{r} 24 \\ -17 \\ \hline 7 \end{array} \quad
\begin{array}{r} 74 \\ -62 \\ \hline 12 \end{array} \quad
\begin{array}{r} 48 \\ -12 \\ \hline 36 \end{array} \quad
\begin{array}{r} 37 \\ -18 \\ \hline 19 \end{array}
$$

Page 122

$$
\begin{array}{r} 59 \\ -48 \\ \hline 11 \end{array} \quad
\begin{array}{r} 26 \\ -12 \\ \hline 14 \end{array} \quad
\begin{array}{r} 38 \\ -38 \\ \hline 0 \end{array}
$$

128